A GUIDE ON DOING BUSINESS

With the State in South Africa

Volume 1

By Tebogo K Monoametsi

For permission requests, write to the author at their email address:
Tebogo K Monoametsi
Email: tkmonoametsi@conteb.co.za

Published by The Golden Goose Institute (Pty) Ltd
Website: www.thegoldengooseinstitute.com
Email: info@thegoldengooseinstitute.com

Cover design by Motsanaphe Morare (Azaniainini@gmail.com)
Interior design by The Golden Goose Institute (Pty) Ltd
Editor: Soneni Sonia Dube (sdube@thegoldengooseinstitute.com)
Proofreader: Soneni Sonia Dube (sdube@thegoldengooseintitute.com)

ISBN: 978-0-6397-9460-0

For further information about the author or their publications, please
contact the author via email.

First Edition: 2023

FOREWORD

Moremogolo go betlwa wa taola wa motho o a ipetla

Gaopalelwe Walter Molelekwa would like to complete this foreword in my mother tongue to reflect my full appreciation for the privilege that Mr Tebogo Monoametsi afforded me to read this brilliant ground breaking work *ke a leboga nkgonne*.

This book is not written by someone green or what is called in the law profession 'n *kort broek* advocate.' Mr Tebogo Monoametsi is a seasoned Supply Chain Management practitioner and director with practical and academic credentials to back up this book, and the academics achieved at a level 9, with an *MBL majoring in Supply Chain and MBA majoring in Agile Supply Chain Management.*

This book is written in a straightforward and simple language and contains practical information that will assist the current and aspiring entrepreneurs to understand the procurement environment in the South African Public Sector. It will enable the current and prospective entrepreneurs, the current and aspiring Supply Chain Management practitioner and Supply Chain Management academics to understand the government procurement legislative environment and practice.

This book clearly outline and simplifies all the basic government procurement Legislation and Regulations. A clear interpretation of what some of the SCM concepts linguistically mean according to government SCM officials and practitioners is provided in this book.

This book is a ground breaker, because there has never been such an attempt to unselfishly share the insights of government procurement practice and its complex processes. It shares the lived and daily experiences of a Supply Chain Management practitioner and their decision making process. It provides the perspectives of why some entrepreneurs fail to enter the lucrative procurement of government and provides some advice on how to enter these procurement opportunities.

In my personal capacity, and with my practical experience and exposure to government procurement, I vouch and recommend that you read and digest the contents of this book and its sequel should one have the thirst to be an astute, sustainable and successful entrepreneur and a diligent Supply Chain Management practitioner or academic.

... Rutang bana ditaola, lo seye natso Badimong

DEDICATION

I dedicate this book to all the business people who work hard daily, never knowing where their next meal will come from yet keep on going. You are the future of this country. The creation of employment and sustainability of business depends on you.

ACKNOWLEDGEMENTS

I give all the praise and glory to God for the guidance in writing this book.

I would also like to thank my family, friends, and colleagues who supported me through this journey and all the people who will bless this initiative and support it by purchasing the book.

TABLE OF CONTENTS

ABBREVIATIONS

AG:	Auditor General
B-BBEE:	Broad-based Black Economic Empowerment
CIDB:	Construction Industry Development Board
CIPC:	Companies and Intellectual Property Commission
CSD:	Central Supplier Database
DTI:	Department of Trade and Industry
HDI:	Historically Disadvantaged Individuals
MFMA:	Municipal Finance Management Act
NHBRC:	National Home Builders Registration Council
OCPO:	Office of the Chief Procurement Officer
PFMA:	Public Finance Management Act
PPPFA:	Preferential Procurement Policy Framework
PPR:	Preferential Procurement Regulations
SANAS:	South African National Accreditation System
SARS:	South African Revenue Services
SCM:	Supply Chain Management

INTRODUCTION

M ost people refer to doing business with the government as tendering while others refer to it as a source of corruption. Still, others refer to persons who do business with the government as "tenderpreneurs". Whatever you choose to call it, the truth is that government plays a huge role in business, enabling economic growth and income distribution through massive spending. For instance, the budgeted amount for goods and services - excluding state-owned entities and municipalities revenue collection - for the year 2023/2024 has been set as R305.2 billion (*National Treasury of South Africa, Budget Review 2023*). This sum excludes employee remuneration and simply indicates that it must be spent through procurement.

Apart from the compensation of employees and possibly other minor expenditures such as electricity bills, all allocated monies provided to state organisations and entities for service delivery must be used for purchase. As a result, and because the government is a major purchaser of products and services, there is a significant opportunity for businesses to enter that market. All else being equal, and assuming there is no alleged corruption with the mechanisms being fair according to the prescripts of the Republic's Constitution, Section 217, state procurement should help develop the country's enterprises and should play a vital role in job creation.

In this book, I will discuss some principles for tapping into that business environment and maybe opening your eyes to what is allowed and forbidden, particularly when seeking to conduct business with provincial governments, municipalities, and state-owned businesses. The state is a highly regulated environment, and business people are no exception to the regulations. Understanding how to comply and capitalise on available opportunities comes at the cost of educating yourself and learning daily what the regulations entail and how to fulfil them.

Nobody embarks on a journey without first determining and preparing what they will require. For example, if you want to go on vacation, you must first decide where you want to travel. How will you get there? What are the prerequisites for getting there? How much money will you require? Where will you get the necessary documents? All those minor elements must be considered in order to have a successful and enjoyable holiday. Similarly, as an entrepreneur or business person, you will require a road map. Most business people think of registering a company as the initial step, while others know exactly what they want to achieve but do not know how to do it. The cliché of all of this in South Africa is that the majority of people want to actually build such businesses in order to have any or specific opportunities within the state - either through the supply and delivery of commodities or the provision of a service.

The assumption I will make is that you have registered your company and that you have goods or services to offer. Another assumption I shall make while I write this is that everything is fair, transparent, equitable, competitive, and cost-effective, as intended by Section 217 of the South African Constitution. We will be discussing the magic touch aspect that will set you apart and expand your business, or at the very least get you on the path to the destination you're aiming for.

Let us embark on this adventure to discover how to progress from plain survival business etiquette to the great business ethics and procedures of a sustainable business.

PART I

UNDERSTANDING THE GOVERNMENT TENDER SYSTEM

Chapter 1

THE RIGHT MINDSET

There is a Chinese proverb that states,
"A man without a smiling face must not open a shop".

The mindset of a company is its most powerful weapon. That comes with the desire to be your own boss. Others are inspired by something else, while others are motivated by a wonderful concept they wish to implement. Whatever the motive for starting a business, the truth is that the mentality of a business person must be in the proper state. Undoubtedly, you will make many mistakes, some of which will be costly while others will be advantageous, but the reality remains that those mistakes must be learnt from.

When your thinking is clear and you have objectives for what you want to do, by when, and why, the 'how' portion becomes the difficulty you must conquer. Discipline is a vital mindset for any business person. Without discipline, you will waste a lot of time on unimportant things while ignoring essential things where you may genuinely make little improvements to expand your business.

As one wise man once stated, failing to plan is planning to fail; therefore, I am creating this book to ensure that the attitude to succeed is nurtured and developed rather than an idle mind. Another wise person stated that your thoughts must be put to good use daily, just as you choose your clothes every day. Choose carefully what your mind spends its time on.

Promoting Your Business

I like to joke with many small or emerging business owners that your product is not Tupperware or a mining company, thus you must do the groundwork every day. Tupperware does not advertise on television, yet it is almost guaranteed that it is in every or most households. Nevertheless, Tupperware has recently experienced difficulties and must adjust its marketing strategy or face bankruptcy. Such a product already has a brand, a strong word-of-mouth referral network, and a good reputation for quality. As an emerging entrepreneur, you still need to knock on a lot of doors; some will not open, others will open but not have what you need inside, while other doors you will have to push open, and others will wait for your knock. Every day, your mind must be prepared to accept that risk. "*You can't have a million-dollar dream with a minimum wage work ethic*," Stephen C. Hogan once said.

We live in a technological age where everything is at our fingertips thanks to smartphones. You must have an email address to register a business. Now, your phone must have data, or you need to know where to get free data if you are unfortunate enough not to have data. Instead of using social media, a business person will use their data to hunt for opportunities. Not that social media is terrible, but if you use it for likes and to see what is hot or hilarious today, your data will be squandered on things that will not help you achieve your goals. If social media is important to your business, invest in it and go for it.

Now that we've gotten that out of the way, we know that our data must be used efficiently for prospecting or promoting the business. Therefore, everything you post must place you on the map so that others know what service you can offer them. Remember that you are not Tupperware, so you must advertise yourself.

Managing Your Hours

Everyone has the same number of hours in a day; the difference is how we spend them. However, those hours are delivered daily and cannot be banked, stored, or delayed. Allow this to sink in. Time lost or squandered can never be recovered. When you wake up, divide your time according to how you want to spend it and see if you can complete half of your goals. Clear your mind and make sure you are disciplined enough to meet at least three of the goals, excluding sleep time because the body needs sleep. Even if you strive hard not to sleep, the body will simply shut down and tell you that you must sleep.

At this point, you may be wondering what all these difficult aspects of one's mindset have to do with conducting business with the state. The answer is everything. If your perspective is not that of a business person, you will just lose valuable time that could have been spent on more helpful activities that you enjoy.

A simple breakdown of a normal 24 hours is as below:

- **Sleep:** According to wise people who research our bodies' effectiveness, you require at least 8 hours of sleep per day. This is the time when your body heals and recovers from the rigours of daily life. Assuming you do not have any stress or disease that interferes with getting a decent night's rest, there is no reason for you not to get the full 8 hours of sleep. Longer sleep hours sound pleasant, but are they beneficial? You make the call. I usually think that I'll sleep enough when I'm dead, but my father always says that because I'm black, even when I die, I'll have to work because family will come to the gravesite and make sure I hear everything they say. I'm just hoping that I will ignore them and sleep in peace when that time comes.

- **Work:** A working person must work an average of at least 8 hours per day. When you add that to the 8 hours of sleep, you've already absorbed 16 hours of the day.
- **Miscellaneous:** Now you have 8 hours in your daily bank account of life left over, assuming no drama and a routine day. This time is dedicated to job preparation, eating, going to the gym, driving or taking public transportation, and so on.

A business person's attitude cannot function with the simplicity of a regular worker. Sleep is nearly unheard of, especially for a small business owner, though the body forces you to sleep or else you would become ill. An entrepreneur structures their time differently from the moment their feet hit the ground after sleeping for 4 to 6 hours (*I'm referring to an ambitious and industrious entrepreneur here*). Do not be deceived by folks who have easy things come their way; they make up less than 1% of the field of business. The rest of the time, hard work is the order of the day. That hard work must now be clever, accurate, and timely, and must bring value, even if it is riddled with rejections. Rejection indicates that you attempted. Remember that failure only happens to those who attempt; those who do not try cannot fail. Therefore, make failure and rejection your most important teachers. If you do not learn from your mistakes, you will make the same ones again. A lesson is never finished until it is learnt.

An entrepreneur understands the importance of time. By the end of each day, they realise that they require more time in a day. Successful company owners who have grown, established, and can afford certain things buy time by delegating certain tasks to others so that they can devote more time to vital tasks that they have prioritised. What exactly do I mean? I'll give you an example. Paying someone to mow the grass and wash your car will buy you an hour or two to focus on your most critical tasks, but if you are not a gym goer, doing these yourself will result in unallocated time for gym use. However, keep in mind that almost all outsourcing is dependent on budget/affordability.

An entrepreneur who sleeps for 6 hours has two hours to spare for the gym, breakfast preparation, and travel. You must train yourself to be like an early bird who catches the fattest worm. Meaning, accomplish things early in the morning when the brain is fresh unless you are the sort who functions better after 10 a.m. and coffee. Binge-watching TV is not appropriate for a business person. According to healthshots.com, binge-watching can cause the following:

(1) It can make you feel lonely. Binge-watching is a great way to unwind and disconnect from the world whenever you need a break.

(2) Insomnia. Sleep is critical to human health.

(3) Cognitive issues.

(4) Depression.

(5) Mood disturbance and behaviour changes.

Furthermore, you need to focus on building networks, therefore the individuals you associate with must provide value to your life or business; choose them wisely.

A business person, especially one who is new or in the early stages, must always remember that the clock is for individuals who are comfortable, not for you. When you get up and open your phone, the first thing you must do is check your emails and then access the tender website (www.etender.gov.za) or any other opportunity websites. Check your calendar or plan for the day's activities. Set aside time to network if you have no business to attend to. Visit state organisations and inquire about available opportunities. Be present, felt, known, and committed to your company since it is your vision, bread and butter.

Let us now go into the specifics of what you need to know to do business with the state. I'll take you on a journey to learn and comprehend how the state works and what you need to know to enter that place successfully. One rapper/musician by the pseudonym 50 Cent said, "Get rich or die trying". I'm going to assume that the ultimate reason you're in business is to create wealth or become rich or sustainable.

Chapter 2

WHY CSD?

When you intend to do business with the state in South Africa, it is a requirement that you register on the CSD. CSD is an acronym for Central Supplier Database. It is accessible via a website: www.csd.gov.za.

The purpose of the CSD is to maintain a database of organisations, institutions, and individuals who can provide goods and services to the government (www.csd.gov.za). The system is designed with the objective of reducing duplication of effort and cost for suppliers and the government while enabling electronic processes (www.ncpo.treasury.gov.za). You have the choice of registering your business yourself or going in person to the CSD office at Treasury, where you will receive assistance in doing so. Avoid paying someone to register you because doing so on the CSD is **entirely free**.

The following assumptions are made for this step to be successful:

- You have registered a company at CIPC (Companies and Intellectual Property Commission);
- You have received your tax number from SARS (South African Revenue Service);
- You have a valid cellphone with a number and email address; and
- Have also registered a valid bank account with any of the South African Banks.

The CIPC gives you the company number, SARS your tax number, and the bank provides you with a bank account. These are the critical things you need for you to be able to start registering on CSD.

The documents required for each type of business to be able to register on CSD include:

Supplier Type	Supplier Sub-Type	Which ID type is required from the Supplier?	Which tax number is required
Individual	Individual	SA ID or Foreign ID number or Foreign Passport number	Income Tax Reference Number if ID type is SA ID number
Individual	Sole Proprietorship	If a Foreign ID number or Foreign Passport number is provided, a Work Permit number is provided if applicable.	PAYE Refence number and VAT number is optional
Foreign Company	Foreign Company	Foreign Company Registration number or International Securities Identification Number (ISIN)	Optional PAYE Reference number or VAT number or Income Tax Reference Number
Intervivos Trust	Intervivos Trust	SA Trust Registration number or Foreign Trust Registration number	Income Tax Reference Number if ID type is SA ID number
Non Profit Organisation (Department of Social Development)	Non Profit Organisation (Department of Social Development)	Non-profit organization number	Income Tax Reference number of the trust
CIPC Company	Public Company (Ltd); State Owned Company (SOC LTD); Non Profit Company (NPC); Private Companies (Pty)(Ltd); Personal Liabilities Companies (INC); Close Corporations; Primary Co¬operative; Tertiary Co-operative; Limited by Guarantee; Transvaal Ordinance; Unlimited; Non-Profit External Company; External Company	SA Company/ CC Registration number	Income Tax Reference number, PAYE Reference number and Vat number is optional
Unincorporated Body of Persons	Partnership; Statutory Body; Join Ventures; Consortium; Section Companies; Voluntary Associations; Retirement Fund	SA ID of main partner or International Securities Identification number(ISIN)	PAYE Refence number and VAT number or Income Tax Refence number
Source: *www.csd.gov.za*			

Once you are on the website, click 'Register', and follow all the fields/prompts, making sure you remember your passwords (Hint! Take a picture of that screen with your phone or write down everything in your private diary but keep such safe). Please note that a full CSD report/certificate from the day of registration takes about three (3) to four (4) working days for applications that are complete and compliant.

NB: Remember to always acknowledge the prompt messages when you log into CSD for you to be able to continue further. Also, know where your local treasury offices are if you need speedy assistance. You can check on this website for the different provincial contact details:

https://secure.csd.gov.za/Feedback/ProvincialContacts

To finalise your entire registration process, the information that you will be required/prompted to complete in terms of the different categories in the CSD will be as follows:

• Supplier Identification
• Supplier Industry Classification Information/Commodities
• Supplier Contact Information
• Supplier Address Information
• Supplier Bank Account
• Supplier Tax Information
• Supplier Accreditation Information
• Supplier B-BBEE Information
• Ownership Information

Let's unpack each of them further.

Supplier Identification

In this category, a CSD or supplier number will be provided, and it starts with 'MAAA'. The company registration number (CIPC) will be displayed with the legal and trading name of the business. The legal name is the name registered at CIPC, while the trading name is the name your company uses or is known as when conducting its business. The two can be the same. The business status will show if the company is in business or deregistered, or if it is in the process of deregistration. Other information in this category will be: country of origin, if you have a bank account, total annual turnover, and financial year start date.

The most important information for government officials in Supply Chain Management (SCM) to investigate is the part that says *'restricted supplier'*. If your company is restricted, you will not be requested a quote or will be disqualified from competitive bidding. This can happen for any other reason that you may possibly know of, or are aware of. However, if you are not aware of any reason for the restriction, then you must contact your nearest Treasury office. As a business person, you must conduct your affairs in a professional manner; deliver as per the order, on time, and of the quality required. It is within your duty as a citizen of South Africa to avoid any fraudulent activities while conducting your business as this might lead to your company being restricted to doing business with the state.

It is your duty as a business person to check your CSD status daily. If your business status is showing anything other than 'In Business', you might be asked by the requesting SCM officials/ state organisation to submit evidence or reasons why it is reflecting as such. Normally, you must be provided some time to respond (like 7 days), but that depends on the urgency of what they require.

In a tender process, which I will explain in the latter relevant section, the process takes long to conclude so you will be written a formal email/letter asking you to submit information regarding your status. This happens normally if you are a potential winning bidder, however, in a quotation scenario you *might* be informed but note that it is solely your responsibility to check and manage your company including the CSD.

Supplier Industry Classification Information/ Commodities

In this category, the government wants to know what you can do for them. This is where you state your commodities, or the kind of service you are offering. The classification information will be split between the main group, division, and core industry.

If you are in business, you should know what you're doing, right? You would be shocked at how many people register companies and claim to be doing everything. Some people start a business to escape the scourge of poverty, some have a wonderful concept, others are just seeking any opportunity, and still, others have always wanted to be their own boss. Whatever your purpose for starting a business, the fact is that you cannot do everything. To be practical and realistic, you must first determine the specialised market you wish to enter. If you are performing supply and delivery, which is what most newly registered business persons do, especially those who want to do business with the state, you must state what you are supplying or, at the very least, what you specialise in delivering.

If you supply stationery, for example, you must know where you can stock at a low cost and resell it to the state at a suitable markup. A markup is the amount of money you add to the cost of a product to make a profit. This will be explained more in a quotation section. We're still on CSD; I was simply demonstrating the significance of this section and how it relates to the overall picture of doing business with the government.

Supplier Contact Information

The state wants to know who you are and how to contact you or send you requests. This is the category that details information such as your name, surname, cellphone number, email address, and preferred method of communication. I cannot overemphasise the importance of keeping this information up to date and correct. A tip for you: your method of preferred communication must be email. This is to ensure everything comes written, traceable, and verifiable. This is purely to protect you from fraud and scams. You can put more than one contact person but can only put one preferred contact person.

Supplier Address Information

This category is about your location. The preferred address is the address you are operating your business at. This is mostly your head office or any other office you choose to be the preferred address. You can add other addresses and won't be limited, unfortunately, you are only limited to one preferred address. The preferred address is normally the one registered at CIPC, however, you can choose which one is the preferred address to you based on your proximity to doing business.

Most companies get too excited about this information and go wild. You will find a company having more than nine addresses while in South Africa we only have nine Provinces. It is not wrong since some provinces have a large geographical landscape, and it makes sense for your company to be closer to where you render the services, and where you can afford the rentals. Note that when government officials select companies on CSD, they also choose the local address that is stated as the preferred address. So, you might have a company address in Limpopo, but your preferred address is in Gauteng. Therefore, you will mostly stand a chance of receiving quotes from Gauteng state organisations than Limpopo. Having many addresses is not a problem but whether they are valid business addresses that can be verified is a whole different question that can lead to your business losing some points allocated for locality.

Supplier Bank Account

The bank account you record here is the account of your business or preferably that you want to be paid into for services rendered. It must be valid and still in existence. The details recorded here must be exactly as the bank has captured them. If the bank made an error with the account holder's name, you must capture it on the CSD with that error. *The best way to ensure you don't make mistakes is to obtain a bank confirmation letter from your bank and use the details as they appear on the letter. Those who are tech-savvy can use their banking app to download that bank confirmation letter.*

Verification of the bank details on CSD can take up to four days. Should it by any chance take longer than that and you have captured everything correctly, you can contact Treasury at csd@ treasury.gov.za with your CSD number (the 'MAAA' one), as well as your bank confirmation letter for assistance. When the banking details have been verified, it will show the status as 'Verification Succeeded'.

The correct and verified banking details make it easier for you to be paid on time after rendering a service. Remember that in business, cash flow is very important for sustaining the business, therefore you don't want to offer services for free. So always check your CSD report to ensure your information is still correct and curb any fraud should anyone have access to your details/profile and change your bank details.

Supplier Tax Information

The tax number you received from SARS is required in this category. If you are VAT registered, your VAT number will also be in this section. CSD interlinks with SARS, meaning that your tax status can be verified on CSD without having to obtain a tax certificate. However, the tax status changes regularly depending on your compliance with SARS requirements, therefore, always have access to SARS to obtain a Tax Pin which can be used to verify the status on the SARS website if the information on CSD does not match your expectations.

Remember, doing business with the state requires your tax affairs to be in order; by this I mean you need to be compliant. The state budget is funded by taxes; therefore, one cannot expect to obtain business from the state while they do not pay their taxes. This is just on a lighter but truthful note. It is like biting the hand that feeds you. The regulations of government state that any business that intends to or does business with the state must be tax complaint before being awarded a tender, where tender means 'price quote or competitive bid' (*National Treasury Instruction No 09 of 2017/2018*).

Supplier Accreditation Information

If your company is in the construction industry and is registered with the Construction Industry Development Board (CIDB), your information will be verified in this section. Your CIDB grading, active status, and expiry date of certification will be reflected here. I will detail the CIDB part in the latter section on tips to succeed in competitive bids.

Supplier B-BBEE Information

The Broad-based Black Economic Empowerment (B-BBEE) Act, No. 53 of 2003, as amended, aims to advance economic transformation, and enhance the economic participation of black people in the South African economy. The B-BBEE scorecard measures a level of compliance against the five (5) elements, namely: Ownership, Management Controlled Employment Equity, Skills Development, Enterprise and Supplier Development, and Socio-economic Development. I will not expand on this since it has been in existence for a while.

The level of contribution status will be reflected in this section. We all know that this has not been implemented efficiently and is subject to abuse and collusion, not to mention fronting. To avoid many problems as a business, have a SANAS (South African National Accreditation System) accredited agent to assess your company and provide you with a B-BBEE certificate that's valid when applying for any tender (price quote or competitive bid). There is also an easier way provided by the Department of Trade and Industry (DTI), whereby you can print, complete a form then certify and commission it for your B-BBEE status. The commissioning can be done by any commissioner of oaths, like at the police station. Note that this certificate is only valid for two (2) years.

Ownership Information

The demographic information is detailed here; the name and surname of the owner/s, their identification numbers if they are individuals, whether they are South African citizens or not, their ethnic group, gender, youth, disabled, military veteran, rural area and township information.

The important information on individual directors reflected here will be their status (active or not), whether they are a restricted supplier, government employee verification, and the companies they are involved in. This information if it is negative without any substantive evidence can lead your quote or competitive bid to be disqualified. Please check this information constantly to ensure there is nothing negative.

Chapter 3

TYPES OF COMMON PROCUREMENT IN THE TENDER PROCESS

There are different kinds of procurement that are used by the state. Some are used to collect information on what business they can offer, some for competitive purposes with the intention of awarding the contract to the best qualifying service provider, while other procurement is to create a database where service providers can be selected from. I will be detailing those different kinds of procurement below.

Tender

The new Preferential Procurement Regulations (PPR), 2022 define a tender as a written offer in the form determined by an organ of state in response to an invitation to provide goods or services through price quotations, a competitive tendering process, or any other method envisaged in legislation. You will note that with the prior regulations, tender and quotations were defined differently.

Tender used to be any procurement over the Rand value of one million rands (R1 000 000) under the Public Finance Management Act (PFMA), 1999, while under the Municipal Finance Management Act (MFMA), 2003, a tender was any procurement over the Rand value of two hundred thousand rands (R200 000.00). I'm just notifying you of the new definition of tender in the current regulation, which doesn't differentiate between quotations and competitive bidding.

I will later explain all the thresholds so you can get a clear picture of where your focus and strengths need to be, so that you can set your goals correctly before you apply for any tender. I essentially don't want you to send a CV to the hospital applying to be a Doctor (Physician) while your qualifications reflect that you are a Mechanical Engineer. Punch within your weight, and don't waste time on things you don't qualify for. Desperation is not appealing, neither is time-wasting or wasting energy in such a huge paperwork environment which can be very costly.

RFI (Request for Information)

An RFI is used when the solution to a business problem is not immediately evident or clearly defined. The RFI is used to gather information, NOT to select or award any company with the tender. You cannot use this submission as a reference for work done for the state. This is where you market your business and inform the state of what you can offer them in comparison to their needs. How will it benefit them in terms of cost and value?

The Supply Chain Management Unit join forces with the end user who is the customer to clearly describe the problem, solicit external expertise regarding how to solve the problem, and study proposed solutions. The reason for this type of procurement is purely to look for the best solution available for the state.

RFP (Request for Proposal)

An RFP is used when the state organisation understands the business problem and what is needed to solve it, including specifications and procedures. Price is usually not the determining factor in the evaluation of an RFP. Factors such as quality, service, and reputation are also taken into consideration.

Before you submit your proposal, make sure you understand the problem. Check if you actually qualify to provide the solution. In other words, read the document thoroughly. Identify what extra help you are going to require for such a problem and initiate joint ventures or partnerships, or even a memorandum of understanding (MOU) with those you are bringing on board. An RFP can result in an award if it meets all the requirements and provides the best solution the organ of state desires. Note that it is also a time-consuming exercise that equates to a lottery - similar to tendering with no guarantees.

RFQ (Request for Quote)

An RFQ is used to obtain pricing, delivery information, as well as terms and conditions from suppliers. In this case, requestors have a clear understanding of what they need, including requirements and specifications. To procure the exact product or service needed, the customer/ end-user provides the Supply Chain Management Unit with as much information as possible, including complete specifications, quantities, and delivery.

The regulations do not allow such requests to be brand specific unless in exceptional circumstances that can be justifiable. This is purely to protect you as a business person to shop around for the most economical, cost-effective and quality product without affecting your profit margins while saving the state some costs. We will come to the profit margins and things that make a lot of service providers/tenderers to not be awarded or considered.

Unsolicited Proposals

An unsolicited proposal means any proposal received by an institution outside the normal procurement process that is not an unsolicited bid (a submission that must be innovative, unique, and provided by a sole supplier) (*National Treasury Practice note no 11 of 2008/2009*). This simply means an instance where service providers offer products that were not solicited through a normal procurement process.

I will not dwell much on this but just to inform you that if you have a product or service for which you believe you are the only one who can offer it, then you can submit it to the organ of state you have identified and highlight that they will need that kind of service. Note that they will be duty-bound to test the market to ensure that the product or service you are proposing is not offered elsewhere or that there is an even better one. The product must be innovative, unique, and must be exceptionally beneficial, or have serious cost advantages. It will also depend on the state organisation's budget and other factors. Note that an accounting officer/authority is not obliged to consider an unsolicited bid. So do your proper research for such a proposal and hope for the best.

Public–Private Partnership (PPP)

This is a commercial transaction between a state institution and a private party/company whereby the private party/company performs a state institutional function on behalf of the state institution. The private party/company assumes substantial financial, technical, and operational risks in connection with the performance of the state institutional function and/or use of state property by way of consideration to be paid by the state institution from the revenue generated. Alternatively, the private party/company charges the state institution or charges fees collected from customers or service providers on behalf of the state institution.

This is a tedious and time-consuming procurement that needs a whole lot of steps. If you are a business person and interested in such, please familiarise yourself with Treasury Regulation 16, from

16.1 to 16.10, along with any other relevant instruction note applicable to this.

Procurement Done by Another Organ of State (PFMA and MFMA)

The Treasury Regulations for PFMA state that the accounting officer or accounting authority may, on behalf of the department, constitutional institution, or public entity, participate in any contract arranged by means of a competitive bidding process by any organ of state, subject to the written approval of such organ of state and the relevant contractor. (*Treasury regulation 16A.6.6*)

While the Municipal Supply Chain Management Regulations for MFMA expands it by saying that the supply chain management policy may allow the accounting officer to procure goods or services for the municipality or municipal entity under a contract secured by another organ of state, but only if that contract has been secured by the other organ of state by means of a competitive bidding process applicable to that organ of state.

The MFMA regulations further state that there must be no reason to believe that the contract was incorrectly procured. That there are demonstrable discounts or benefits for the municipality or entity to take such a contract. That the other organ of state and the provider (service provider) have consented to such procurement in writing. (*Municipal Supply Chain Management Regulation; Section 32*)

There are a few things one must note for such a contract to be successful, be it PFMA or MFMA. There must be an identifiable benefit for such a contract, not a simple lack of planning or avoidance of going on a public tender. It must not have been irregularly procured or even suspected of such. Preferably, it should have been audited and not found wanting by the Auditor General, for any state organisation or entity to consider such a contract. This could be a good shortcut for you as a business person but tantamount to chaos for the state organisation you have a contract with if your company is wanted by all state organisations for the same service that you tendered for. You will have to examine your capacity and capability including reputational damage for state capture.

Databases/Panels

This is a form of a tender or RFI but without financial implications. The state organisations might have intentions to collect several service providers into their own database, to be able to use for procurement challenges they may face. Remember CSD is the regulated database, therefore any panel or database advertised must clearly state that only CSD-registered companies will be considered. There will be additional requirements that must be met for your company to be included in that database. The database must be advertised publicly and must not be unfair to other potential applicants in terms of strict functionality requirements.

The main reason for state organisations opting for an additional database while the CSD exists is because they have certain targets and goals they have to meet within their provinces and or municipalities, like the development of certain groups of suppliers/ service providers and also identifying potential sub-contractors from the pool of EMEs (Exempted Micro Enterprises with an annual turnover of R10 million) or QSEs (Qualifying Small Enterprises with a turnover of R10 million or more but less than R50 million). The other technicalities are verified and checked before you are entered into the database, thereby ensuring that when the competition period comes, the period is lessened since the tender period is quite a long one where a month of that gets wasted during the advertisement period of 21 to 30 days.

Each state organisation will prescribe from their supply chain policy how procurement will be done once you are appointed into the database. Note that the procurement period might be short since they will only be inviting your company on a closed bid, but from the panel. It is wiser for state organisations to make such panels/databases competitive instead of just allocating work from it just because the company is already in the database.

Transversal Tenders/Contracts (RT Contracts)

These are contracts negotiated for the government by Treasury wherein departments can buy from them instead of negotiating a new contract. They operate like databases/panels but with prices. As a business person, you need to be checking the tender website to see if there are no RT contracts advertised by Treasury to broaden your exposure. RT contracts are managed by the Office of the Chief Procurement Officer (OCPO). Provincial Treasuries can arrange their own RT contracts for goods or services required on a repetitive basis by one or more participating institutions. The capacity and mandate to manage such rest solely with the Provincial Treasury. (*Treasury Regulation 16A6.5*)

There are different commodities on RT contracts. They are designed to simplify the procurement process and negotiate average prices that will save costs for the state. Service providers get vetted for cost and quality. Before issuing a tender on the e-Tender portal, the state organisation must check if the commodities they require are not catered for in any of the RT contracts. You must always be on alert to check the e-Tender website and Treasury adverts for such an opportunity as a business person, then apply to be in the RT contract.

Limited Bidding Methods

If in a specific case where it is impractical to invite competitive bids, the accounting officer or accounting authority may procure the required goods or services by other means, provided that the reasons for deviating from inviting competitive bids are recorded and approved by the accounting officer or accounting authority (*Treasury Regulation 16A6.4*). The following types of limited bidding methods will be applicable:

- *Multiple source bidding*

This method is used in the case of limited competition where only a few prospective bidders are allowed to make a proposal. Some databases are operated in this manner, but the bidders have already been through the process of public tender before they were in a database. However, you might find some service providers, like cellphone operators, competing with each other since it's only a few of them, hence there is an RT contract for them.

- *Single source bidding*

In this case, only one amongst a few prospective bidders is requested to make a proposal after a transparent and equitable pre-selection process has been followed. This can happen where a two- stage bid was implemented, under which first the unpriced technical proposals based on a conceptual design or performance specifications are invited. This is subject to commercial clarifications and adjustments, and followed by amended bidding documents and technical proposals. The price proposal will be in the second stage.

• *Sole source bidding and sole supplier*

This only happens when a service provider has patent rights or sole distribution rights. They are the only ones who can provide the service or goods, therefore there is no competition in the market. Eskom for example, even though there is potential competition, is solely regulated in their favour. Another example would be Microsoft. The world is evolving and eliminating such monopolies, therefore, such procurements will be a thing of the past soon, as competitors are entering all these spaces and regulations are being relaxed towards fair global markets. Documentary proof must exist that the specific supplier is a sole distributor or has the sole rights for a specific commodity.

• *Emergency/urgent procurement*

These are cases where immediate action is required and necessary to avoid a dangerous or risky situation or misery. The accounting officer/authority may engage in procurement by means of negotiation when there is an urgent need for the goods/ works or service and where the bidding process would be impractical, provided the circumstances giving rise to an urgency/ emergency were unforeseeable by the procuring entity.

Owing to a catastrophic event, there arises a need to urgently procure goods/services or works and it would be impractical to use normal or other available procurement methods because of the time involved in using those methods. In such a situation, a bidder can be identified as a successful bidder through a competitive bidding process which can be approached by the accounting officer/authority to quote and negotiate the price with the bidder.

Chapter 4

THRESHOLDS OF PROVINCIAL GOVERNMENTS AND MUNICIPALITIES

The state defines thresholds as distinct Rand values of procurement from petty cash, quotation, and tender. There is a distinction between the PFMA and the MFMA, although the context is nearly the same. According to Treasury regulation 16A.6.1, "procurement of goods and services, whether by quotation or through a bidding process, must be under the National Treasury's threshold of values."

Following is a clarification of thresholds so that you, as a business person, understand what price range is required when you are invited to bid or quote. I'll start by describing what the 80:20 and 90:10 ratios mean, and then I'll give you the different thresholds for PFMA and MFMA.

The regulations governing the preference point system have been altered from the prior ones, in which 80 or 90 points were assigned to price and 20 or 10 points were assigned to the B-BBEE level respectively. With the new PPR regulation, 2022, 80 and 90 are still the prices, but 20 and 10 are now specified goals. The aims must be defined, documented in the acquiring state organisation's SCM policy, and linked to Historically Disadvantaged Individuals (HDI) in accordance with the Preferential Procurement Policy Framework Act of 2000 (Act no.5 of 2000). (*PPPFA, 2000*)

A Historically Disadvantaged Individual (HDI) means a South African citizen who, due to the Apartheid policy that had been in place, had no franchise in national elections prior to the introduction of the Constitution of the Republic of South Africa, 1983 (Act 110 of 1983) or the Constitution of the Republic of South Africa, 1993, (Act 200 of 1993) ("the interim Constitution"); and/or who is a female;

and/or who has a disability, provided that a person who obtained South African citizenship on or after the coming to effect of the Interim Constitution, is deemed not to be an HDI. (*PPPFA, 2000*)

Any tender (quotation or competitive bid) must include the applicable preference point system in its advertisement. If the organ of state is unsure which price threshold the tender will fall within, they must specify in the bid document that either an 80:20 or 90:10 preference point system will apply and that the highest acceptable tender will be used to decide the applicable preference point system.

The 80:20 Preference Point System

Any acquisition of goods and services for less than R50 million, inclusive of all applicable taxes, will be calculated using the 80:20 preference point method. The preference point system of 80:20 is used for quotations and competitive bids. This can vary depending on whether you are dealing with the municipality (MFMA) or any other state organ (PFMA). The thresholds will be detailed more below after the preference point systems have been clarified. I'm just making sure you understand why such details are included in your invitations or tender documents.

The 80:20 point system is calculated in this manner:

Ps= Points scored for the price of tender under consideration;
Pt= Price of tender under consideration; and
$Pmin$= Price of lowest acceptable tender.

A maximum of 20 points may be awarded to a tender for the specific goal identified for the tender. The points scored for the specific goal must be added to the points scored for price and the total must be rounded off to the nearest two decimal places. The contract must be awarded to the tenderer scoring the highest points unless there are justifiable reasons.

Example of The Calculation			
Details	**Company A**	**Company B**	**Company C**
Price Per Each Company	192,962.60	241,030.00	254,000.00
Total Amount	192,962.60	241,030.00	254,000.00
	PS= $\frac{80\ (1-Pt-Pmin)}{Pmin}$	PS= $\frac{80\ (1-Pt-Pmin)}{Pmin}$	PS= $\frac{80\ (1-Pt-Pmin)}{Pmin}$
	= $80*\frac{(1-(192962.60-192962.60)}{192,962.60}$	= $80*\frac{(1-(192962.60-241030)}{192,962.60}$	= $80*\frac{(1-(192962.60-254000)}{192,962.60}$
Price Points	80.00	60.07	54.69
Specific Points	20.00	10.00	20.00
Total Points Scored	100.00	70.07	74.69

The 90:10 point system is calculated in this manner:

Ps= Points scored for the price of tender under consideration;
Pt= Price of tender under consideration; and
Pmin= Price of lowest acceptable tender.

A maximum of 10 points may be awarded to a tender for the specific goal specified for the tender. The points scored for the specific goal must be added to the points scored for price and the total must be rounded off to the nearest two decimal places. The contract must be awarded to the tenderer scoring the highest points unless there are justifiable reasons.

I'll concentrate on the thresholds that affect PFMA and MFMA because they play the most important roles in the state. You must determine where you will conduct business based on variables such as proximity, capabilities, interest, or whatever motive you may have.

Procurement Thresholds: PFMA

A. *Petty cash (maximum R2000 inclusive of all taxes)*

Accounting officers/authorities may procure goods and services by means of petty cash up to the value of R2000 (inclusive of all applicable taxes) without inviting price quotations or following a bidding process. This process does not have too many restrictions but must always be tightly controlled against abuse. There must be a policy in the state organisation to manage and control petty cash. Care must be made that one item is not procured by using petty cash repeatedly. Such purchases will be added together and if they exceed R10 000 within a short space of time it will be perceived as splitting procurement.

A service provider might be requested to submit a quote for that service without any formal bidding process, and this can happen via telephone. As a business person, it is advisable that this request is sent to you in writing and a formal purchase order be issued. A receipt must be obtained for such a purchase and processing of the claim. This is to safeguard yourself from fraud and ensure that you will be paid. Remember you are running a business, not a charity.

B. *Transactions above the value of R2 000 not exceeding R1 000 000 inclusive of applicable taxes*

All transactions above this threshold have certain prescripts to be adhered to but the key to all compliances is that anyone invited must be registered on CSD. A minimum of three (3) quotes is required but each organ of the state can determine how many quotes they need from which Rand value. For example, R30 000 to R200 000 can be three quotes but more than R200 000 at least five (5) quotes. The law and instruction note No. 2 of 2021/2022 states that three quotes must be given but allows the accounting officer/authorities within their SCM policies to prescribe a different number of invitations and quotes.

I will not go into detail about how many quotes are required by the state institution because that is irrelevant to you as a business person. What is vital are the invite's details/specifications and the due or closing date. As I discuss the quotation process and what to look for when submitting a quote, I will go into greater detail in the following chapters.

C. *Above the transaction value of R1 000 000 inclusive of applicable taxes (competitive bids)*

Accounting officers/authorities must invite open competitive bids for all procurement above R 1 000 000 (inclusive of all applicable taxes). Competitive bids must be advertised in at least the Government Tender Bulletin (suspended for now) and the e-Tender Publication Portal. Accounting officers/authorities may also advertise competitive bids on their institution's website and in any other appropriate media should an accounting officer/authority deem it necessary to ensure greater exposure to potential bidders.

It is your responsibility as a business person to check the websites and the tender bulletin, including the departmental websites for any new advertised opportunities. I will overemphasise this when we talk about competitive bids. For now, the information is for opening your knowledge on when it is a quotation and when is it a competitive bid or what you might famously know as a tender/tendering.

Procurement Thresholds: MFMA

When it comes to municipalities and their entities, the rules differ slightly. The thresholds must be stated in the SCM policy of the municipality.

A. *Petty cash (maximum R2000 inclusive of all taxes)*

The municipal supply chain policy will stipulate the conditions for the procurement of goods and services by means of petty cash. Receipts must always be kept for reconciliation purposes. The procurement process must not be split into petty cash to avoid competitive processes. Similar care and safety must be taken just as in the above prescripts of the PMFA for you as a business person to safeguard yourself from fraud and nonpayment. (*Municipal Supply Chain Regulations 15*)

B. *Transactions above the value of R2 000 not exceeding R10 000 inclusive of applicable taxes*

A written or verbal quotation will be done. It is always best to have your request written because the order can only be issued against a written confirmation by you as the service provider. No order made might result in no payment. I keep saying this to protect you as a business person so that you can be alert of any fraud or being taken for a ride. (*Municipal Supply Chain Regulations 16*)

C. *Transactions above the value of R10 000 not exceeding R 200 000 inclusive of applicable taxes*

A formal written price quotation is acceptable. Now when it comes to this price range, you will notice how the word 'formal' is put forward. This .means that you cannot phone and inform the requesting municipality that you will charge them this much. It will not be accepted.

D. *Transactions above the value of R30 000 not exceeding R 200 000 inclusive of applicable taxes.*

Additional to the requirement of the formal written quotation is that the invite by the municipality for any transactions above the Rand value of R30 000 must be advertised for at least seven (7) days on the website and an official notice board of the municipality or municipal entity. (*Municipal Supply Chain Regulations 18*)

E. *Transactions above the value of R 200 000 inclusive of applicable taxes (competitive bids)*

Competitive bids must be done by means of public advertisement in newspapers commonly circulating locally, the website of the municipality or municipal entity, or any other appropriate way. Competitive bidding will always have bid documents that must be complied with, and time frames adhered to. Unlike quotations, where you can just send minimal information, when it comes to competitive bidding there is a lot of information required which must be complied with. Notice that under the PFMA, this transaction value starts at R1 000 000, however in the MFMA, competitive bids start at R200 000.

Note that the threshold price for local municipality is R300 000, for district municipality it is R200 000, and for metropolitan municipality it is R750 000; all prices inclusive of applicable taxes.

Closing Note

Now that I've outlined the many criteria that will impact you as a business owner. I hope that the facts will help you learn and know how the state works and what makes certain procurement items a tender and others a quotation. You must note that, under the current PPR, 2022, tender might refer to a quote or a competitive offer. Nevertheless, for your convenience and understanding, a tender will continue to be a competitive bid.

PART II

TAKING ACTION IN TENDERING

Chapter 5

QUOTATION PROCESS AND SUBMISSION

Organ of State Steps for Quotation Request

STANDARD QUOTATION PROCESS

Steps	Process	PFMA	MFMA	Things to Lookout For as a Business Person
1	End user/client sends request of a need to the SCM.	Request must not be brand specific.	Request must not be brand specific.	Specifications are to not limit competition (this is for SCM officials)
2	Send to service providers selected from CSD through email and bcc them so they do not see who they are competing against. Alternatively, advertise on the website of the municipality/organ of state.	At least three different suppliers must send quotes back for competition.	At least three different suppliers must send quotes back for competition.	1. Check your emails and visit the websites regularly. Check spam/junk folder as some governmental emails fall through to this folder. 2. Ensure the request is legit and valid. 3. Make sure you understand the specifications and whether the request is worth the time and effort. 4. Ensure you understand all compliance documents required to be submitted and quote correctly. Avoid greed. 5. Check the closing date and time, delivery place, and installation or maintenance.
3	Compare the quotes received while ensuring the quotes are market-related.	Use the applicable PPPFA scores to obtain the winning bidder when the quotations are above R30 000 in value and send the purchase order to the winning bidder.	Use the applicable PPPFA scores to obtain the winning bidder when the quotations are above R30 000 in value and send the purchase order to the winning bidder.	Your duty is to follow up with the requesting state organisation, as to who the winning bidder was and why your quote was not considered. *(Section 217 of the Constitution of the Republic of South Africa allows this)*

As previously indicated, you now have a business and are registered with CSD. You now understand what a quotation is and what a competitive bid is. You've heard about state capture, collusion, corruption, and other phrases associated with state organisations, yet the truth is that you, too, want to do business with the state. You want a piece of the pie, which is so large that it can be shared by virtually everyone. I will now take you through the necessary steps for submitting a quotation to the state.

Let me emphasise this once more: you will not be given business or sometimes an opportunity by the state if you are not registered on CSD. On CSD, your industry classification or what we call commodities is very important for you to be selected. The state institution will go into CSD, and select a commodity, for example, 'printing paper'. They will most likely minimise their selection by choosing an area of the supplier such as 'tax compliant supplier', or 'verified bank account'. They may also select a primary local address, or go to demographics and state that they need youth or women-owned businesses, or businesses owned by people with disabilities. CSD will randomly provide them with the list of service providers within that category and range.

The organ of state will take that list and send the email with the specifications of the print paper they require, together with any additional documents they need you to send back, including the deadline for that submission. Now a business person who doesn't ensure that their email is updated on CSD and that it is monitored will miss this opportunity to submit a quote, and may end up pointing a finger at the state for not being invited to quote. Once again, ensure your details are up to date. Furthermore, you need to regularly check the websites of the departments or municipalities you are interested in doing business with. Go knock at their doors.

Pricing Your Services

Your duty as a service provider is to ensure you understand the request from the state institution and evaluate if you can fulfil it. The best thing is to know where you can obtain what is required at an affordable price without too much additional cost. While at that, you need to know what your markup is. The markup is the price you add on top of the cost to make a profit. A lot of service providers are greedy when it comes to markup. They want to maximise profits, with excuses like, "We might never be called again, so why not increase it now?". Remember, the requester already knows the market in most instances, and they are not willing to over pay for those goods or services. They understand you are in business and you need to make profits, but the key to this is you need to build your profile and reputation of speedy delivery with quality and compliance.

The question you might ask now is what a reasonable markup would be. I cannot dictate that to you, but I can only advice that you at least stay within a 10% to 25% markup. If you are a manufacturer of those goods, you will have to ensure that all the costs for bringing the product to life are calculated including the profit part of it before you can send the quotation. If you are buying from a manufacturer, the delivery cost will possibly be one of your high costs, depending on what you are purchasing. Add all those costs up to know the total cost then add a markup. Once that is done, you can submit your quote. Do not forget to incorporate VAT and other applicable taxes if you are registered for them.

Continuing with the example from the above paragraph, if the state organisation wants a box of printing paper they will not tell you the brand of paper, but they will tell you the size and colour of paper they want. They will also tell you how many boxes if more than one box is required. When you receive such a quotation request, you first assess if it is viable, profitable, or worth the effort and energy.

After that assessment, if you decide to pursue the request, your next step is to check where you are going to obtain that product at a reasonable price. This is called smart business. Just as the state will send to three or more service providers for a quote, your duty is also to go look for the best price. This is what being competitive means; you are not the only one who was requested to provide a quote. The state wants to give you an opportunity to do business with them, but not on a silver platter. You must do the work as well. The smart business person will develop relationships with suppliers and build profiles of being able to obtain some goods on credit and pay for them later.

Let's assume you have the money to buy stock, and you can purchase that box of paper for R500. You didn't spend much on petrol because you could obtain that while doing your household errands right? Wrong. Learn to separate business from your personal expenses. You have spent R40 on transport, so the cost of that paper is R540. The quotation to send will be R540 x 1.1 = R594. Your profit will be R54 if you are successful.

I know what your question is right now. Where does the 1.1 come from? It is a 10% profit you want to make from the 100% cost, so what you do is take the 100% cost, add the 10% profit you want, and then divide the 110% by 100% to get 1.1:

$$(100 + 10) \div 100 = 1.1$$

Alternatively, just say I want 10% profit from the cost i.e. R540 x 10% = R54; then add the R54 to the R540 to get R594. Whichever method you use, make sure you get it right and don't cheat yourself or over-calculate.

If you are VAT registered, always remember to add your VAT in this manner:

R594 x 15% = R89.10
R594 + 89.10 = R683.10

In other words, the cost will be R594 and you add the R89.10 to it which equals R683.10.

Now a smart business person will calculate it in this manner:

R500 x 15% = R75 (VAT) + R40.00 (Transport) + R500
(Original Cost of Paper) = R615.00 (Total Charge)

Underneath the paper cost they will add R40 for transport then the total charge will be R615.

Now compare the two and see who will win this bid. R683.10 vs R615; the writing is on the wall. The smart business person will win purely because they understand the art of business. There is a slip for the R500 cost, but most probably the transport cost doesn't have evidence to provide to SARS, so they charge VAT on what they can get back from SARS. Then you complain about corruption, but it is your business methods which are poor.

Now one might ask, "What if I don't have the money to stock but I am interested in competing for this request for quotation?". You are a business person, you need to know the organisations that provide assistance with such matters. Know what their requirements are, and what their interest rate is but know that all that will impact your R54 profit. If you add up the interest on the cost to ensure you obtain the same profit, then you better be praying heavily that you still quote less than your competitors. Even after quoting less than the competitors who you won't know since they are Bcc'd on email to avoid collusion, the organ of state can still tell you that your price is too high because they already know what the market price should be and they don't want to be accused of failing the state and the constitutional mandate of cost-effectiveness.

Ensuring You Have the Required Documentation

It is not only the price that will make you win the bid. You have to complete all the required returnable documents. All the Standard Bid Document (SBD) forms sent to you must be correctly and accurately completed. Furthermore, your taxes must be compliant. If you have received a quotation for infrastructure or the built environment (construction industry), your Construction Industry Development Board (CIDB) registration must be active and valid. If it involves the built environment, especially housing, your National Home Builders Registration Council (NHBRC) certificate must exist and be valid. You need to ensure that any additional documentation required is completed correctly.

Your quote will be examined for responsiveness and administrative correctness as soon as possible after the closing date. The organ of state will check if your company and its directors are not on the list of restricted bidders/persons or in the register of tender defaulters. Should that be the case, the company will not be considered for further evaluation. If any of the directors are employees of the state without authority, your quote will be disqualified. Should you not disclose this information, and it is later found out, the company might be reported for financial misconduct and the accounting officer/authority will take necessary disciplinary action against the official concerned. You also have to be very careful who you include on your list of staff or employees as that might lead to your bid being disqualified.

Delivering the Goods

Let's say you have won the bid. What is next? Supply what is needed at the speed of lightning if you can. This happens mostly if you have access to funds, access to suppliers whom you stock with, and if the product is available. Deliver the right product required; if you are not sure, ask the SCM officials to confirm. Do not add what is not required or subtract what is required then claim you need to be paid extra. If the order is changed, it must be put in writing including any additions so that you can also be paid for those extras. When you deliver, have your delivery note and invoice always, especially if you need to be paid faster. The state must pay you within 30 days, but nothing restricts you from asking them when they estimate you will be paid so that you can plan your cash flows. If you are paid quicker, even better.

One more thing I forgot to mention is that most organs of state have a walk-in register. In other words, they let service providers record their details for quick invitations and emergency invitations. This is not legal, since CSD is a recognised database. This is just because the practice was always there before the CSD, so they continue to do it. The other reason is that most service providers do not respond on CSD, and the ones on the register are perceived to be hungry because they took their time to market themselves and knocked on the organisation's doors. These are businesses that remember that they are not Tupperware or a mining company, and they manage their daily diary to market themselves. They never get tired of rejection and knocking because they understand the meaning of business.

Closing Notes

I have bombarded you with a lot but have given you some valuable tips:

- Do not overcharge unnecessarily. I write all this assuming that you are not this business person who relies on corruption and that you have inside information. Remember, you will be the same as the person you accuse of corruption if you enable it and motivate it.
- Look at your actions, how you have been quoting, and your business behaviours holistically and be honest with yourself about whether you need to do better or improve.
- Be the best at sales or the best salesperson. If you can't sell it why go into business?
- Remember, Tupperware doesn't need adverts for a reason. You need marketing, pushing, hustling, knocking, and doing whatever it takes to make those sales but avoid being an instigator of corruption.

Taking Action in Tendering

Chapter 6

COMPETITIVE BIDDING/TENDER PROCESS AND SUBMISSION

The competitive bidding or tendering process is motivated/ inspired by the Rand values. The values for the municipalities or municipal entities start at R200 000 but for other organs of state the Rand values start at R1 000 000. Because of the high values, the processes have to be tedious including the requirements. This is not because the state wants to discourage or eliminate small businesses, but they need to realise value for money while obtaining quality services. In this section, I will unpack the competitive bidding process

If you were going to perform renovations in your home, you would not want to spend more than R200 000 without verifying that you are spending it on the correct person and getting the most value for money, would you? Thus, the state follows the same idea because it uses taxpayers' money, which must be spent appropriately. It's sad that we now have many instances of bad workmanship, collusions, and power play that affect and permit corruption, even though we have such stringent laws and regulations in place. I will not linger on the disadvantages, but rather on the processes that can allow you to compete as an acceptable bidder and ensure you comply professionally with minimal to no errors.

The first thing you must do daily is go to the e-Tender website (*www.etenders.gov.za*) and look for tenders that interest you at least three times a day, without fail. Open the tender website as you wake up before you go on social media.

Let me first inform you of the following: the competitive bidding/tender process is subjected to three main committees, namely, the Bid Specification Committee, Evaluation Committee, and Adjudication Committee. The roles of these committees in summary are as follows:

I.   Bid Specifications Committee (BSC)

The Specifications Committee is a standing committee, in which ad hoc members can be roped in with technical know-how of the need or bid in question, accommodating the end user to elaborate further on the need. Their responsibility is to compile the specifications/terms of reference (TOR) for the acquisition of goods or services required by the state organisation and ensure that the funds are available for such procurement.

The decision for advertising the tender on an 80:20 or 90:10 preference system is taken by this committee based on estimated values from their market analysis. Briefing sessions, functionality, pre-qualifications, subcontracting, advertising date, closing date, and local production contents are decided on by this committee. A delegated official/s (chairperson), the committee itself (if delegated), or the accounting officer/authority approves the specification.

II. Bid Evaluation Committee (BEC)

The BEC is a cross-functional committee responsible for evaluating and assessing bids received after an advert is closed. The committee members must not serve on the Bid Adjudication Committee. All bids are evaluated according to the criteria that were advertised on the bid documents including the preference point system (PPPFA) of 80:20 or 90:10. The BEC will check the capability of the bidders to execute the contract (functionality), which will include technical, managerial, and financial perspectives.

This functionality test will extend to checking whether the bid is to the specifications concerning quality, compliance, value for money, experience, and current capacity.

The BEC will also check if:

- the bidders' taxes are compliant,
- whether there is no possibility of fronting,
- past execution of contracts by contacting submitted references,
- if financial statements are audited and fairly present if the bid is over R10 000 000,
- that the bidders are not on the restricted bidders register or tender defaulters register, and
- that the directors or any of their employees are not employees of the state and the bidders are not on a list of the tender defaulters.

They will also check if all the returnable documents required are completed and signed. It is critical that the form of offer, especially in the building industry, is completed correctly in words, Rand value, and signed off otherwise the bid is disqualified since there is no offer, irrespective of whether you have completed the bill of quantity.

The BEC will draft a recommendation to the Bid Adjudication Committee. Care must always be given that the BEC doesn't shift its responsibility of making a recommendation of one bidder by leaving the BAC to decide without sufficient evidence citing that it was impossible for the committee to make only one recommendation. This is because it is the responsibility of the BEC to evaluate and recommend the most competitive bidder to the BAC, and not for the BAC to evaluate or do the BEC's scope of work. The BAC must adjudicate to ensure that the decision arrived at by the BEC was fair and can be defendable in a court of law.

III. Bid Adjudication Committee (BAC)

The BAC is the final committee that will make a recommendation to the accounting officer/authority. They must consider the report and recommendation from the BEC and assess such a recommendation/s. The BAC must consider if the recommendations made by the BEC sufficiently indicate that all relevant factors have been considered and that they are logical, legal, and justifiable according to the relevant information available at the BEC's disposal. All disqualified or nonresponsive bidders must be double-checked to ensure that no bidder was marginalised or no errors were committed. Disqualifications must be defensible in a court of law.

The BAC can differ with the recommendations of the BEC and recommend a different service provider. This must be done with sufficient documented evidence that is justifiable and defensible if it was to be tested in the courts of law. After the BAC assesses all documents, they will make the recommendation to the accounting officer/authority for appointment. Before appointment is made, the CSD report will be drawn to check if your taxes are still compliant. If not, you will be afforded an opportunity to remedy that before you receive the appointment letter. The SCM unit will communicate such information with you and will also be responsible for posting the appointment on the website.

The following are some basic steps for the competitive bid/ tendering process that you should note.

STANDARD COMPETITIVE BIDDING/TENDER PROCESS

Step	Process	PFMA and MFMA	Risks	Things To Look Out For As A Businessperson
1	End user/ client sends a request of a need to the SCM, then it is taken to the Specs Committee.	Compile the specifications.	1. Biased specs. 2. Specs being split to avoid the tender process. 3. Prequalification or functionality being set too high or too low. 4. Specs being designed to suit only certain companies unless the nature of the work dictates the complexity. 5. Advert Date and Closing Date not adhering to regulations. 6. Consultants assisting with specs must be subjected to a code of conduct and must never be indirectly involved in the bidding process.	You have no control here until the bid is advertised.
2	The bid must be advertised on the e-Tenders website(www. etenders.gov. za), the municipal website, and relevant papers for municipal tenders.	A minimum of 21 days advert in e-Tenders and the departmental website for PFMA. A minimum of 30 days advert on the municipal website and other relevant newspapers or public platforms on MFMA.	1. Avoiding public invites by not publishing them. 2. Not counting days correctly and advertising for fewer days than the minimum prescribed days. 3. Inviting bids during periods that are not advised to advertise, such as the builders' holiday period or during December festive season, and ultimately eliminating other competitors.	1. Check websites regularly especially the e-Tenders site (www.etenders.gov.za). 2. Ensure the request is legit and valid. 3. Make sure you understand the specifications. 4. Ensure you understand all compliance documents required to be submitted with the quote/bill of quantity (BOQ). 5. Check the closing date and time.

Step	Process	PFMA and MFMA	Risks	Things To Look Out For As A Businessperson
3	Conduct compulsory briefing session if advertised as such.	1. Record all attendees in the attendance register for compulsory briefing session and send it to everyone or upload it. 2. Record the minutes of the briefing session. 3. Upload and send to all attendees any addendums made during the briefing session.	1. Time frames and venue of the briefing session not clear. 2. Not keeping a register or minutes for the briefing session. 3. Not clearly stipulating addendums and articulating same to attendees.	1. Check the bid document for any briefing sessions. 2. Ensure you attend the briefing session and send a technical person to listen to all the matters raised. 3. Refrain from sending people to your company's briefing session who will not bring accurate information back. 4. Ensure you sign the briefing session register correctly, with all the correct contact details of the company.
4	Close the bid on the date and time stipulated on the bid document and announce the name of the bidders or explain the alternative method.	1. If bids are announced, ensure those present sign the closing register. 2. If they are not announced, ensure the list of bidders is published with their prices within 10 working days.	1. Not closing the bid on time. 2. Accepting late bids without marking them. 3. Bids submitted by courier not correctly signed for. 4. Bids submitted to the wrong departments and accepted later.	1. Ensure you submit your bid on time before the closing date and time. 2. Ensure you sign the register for submitting the bid. 3. If you submit by courier or other person, inform them to sign the name of your company. 4. Check and ask when the bidder's list will be uploaded.
5	Compile a list of submitted bids.	1. Ensure the list has the price, name of the bidder, and address if possible. 2. Put a disclaimer that the lowest price tender is not necessarily the winner. 3. Upload the list on the e-Tenders and state organisations' website.	1. Not recording all bids received. 2. Not uploading the list within 10 working days. 3. Wrong price capturing of bidders uploaded on the website.	1. Ensure your price and names are captured correctly. 2. Compare the briefing register to the list of submitted bids and start weighing your competitors.

Step	Process	PFMA and MFMA	Risks	Things To Look Out For As A Businessperson
6	Submit all the bids for BEC and BAC.	1. Bids must be subjected to BEC and BAC.	1. Incorrect appointment without BEC and BAC checking and recommending. 2. Incorrect evaluation and adjudication of bids. 3. Taking longer than the required 90 days from the closing of the bid to complete the awarding process without requesting permission from the bidders.	1. Wait for the outcomes. 2. Ensure the bids were evaluated within the required time frame of 90 days. 3. Request information about why your bid was not successful so that you can correct your mistakes.

The above table is not comprehensive. A lot goes into the bidding process. I will provide a few tips that are critical in the next chapter that you as a business person might be aware of but have not considered carefully when competing.

PART III

TENDER SYSTEM HACKS

Chapter 7

TIPS TO SUCCEED IN THE COMPETITIVE BIDDING/TENDER PROCESS AND SUBMISSION

The mistakes in the tendering process mostly happen in:

- negligent compliance,
- misleading compliance,
- over/under quoting,
- not checking the documents that you are submitting,
- unreliable or untraceable references,
- not ensuring your documents comply and are still valid,
- not checking the CV's of the employees you list,
- not ensuring there is a memorandum of understanding between your company and the specialist that you have attached CV's of,
- JV agreements that don't make sense,
- lack of compliance documents by the JV partner,
- expired certificates, and
- taxes that are not compliant, among other factors.

Let us begin with the basic things that can set you apart that you may have overlooked in times past when submitting your bid.

A. Obtain or Download the Tender Document

How do you find tenders?

You can obtain public-sector tenders by:

- Accessing the E-Tender website (www.etenders.gov.za).
- Following up on contract notices published in newspapers and trade magazines.
- Getting the government tender bulletin (www.gpwonline.co.za). Note that the publication of tenders is suspended currently on the tender bulletin and e-Tenders is the active site.
- Searching organs of state, municipalities, or department websites.

Once you have selected a tender that you want to compete for, get the tender documents (which are normally downloaded from www.etenders.gov.za) as soon as possible and find out whether and when a compulsory briefing meeting is scheduled. Certain tenders require a compulsory briefing session; if you fail to attend, you may be disqualified from bidding for the tender. Note the place and time of the briefing session/meeting. If it's online, ensure you have adequate data and no electricity cut-offs.

There are sites that specialise in matching and classifying tenders to your exact business requirements by searching e-Tenders, websites, and papers on your behalf, but you will pay a fee for such a service. The services will save you a lot of time by searching numerous websites and scrolling the e-Tenders website on your behalf. My suggestion will be to look for such sites. The few I know are the following but not limited to:

- Online tenders: (www.onlinetenders.co.za)
- SA Tenders: (www.sa-tenders.co.za)

- Tenderkom: (www.tenderkom.com)
- Tender Services: (www.tenderservices.co.za)
- Easy Tenders: (www.easytenders.co.za)
- Tenders on Time: (www.tendersontime.com)
- Tenders HQ: (www.tenderhq.co.za)

If you use these services, you will still have to do the work to ensure they are not missing something you didn't specify as your interest, but that is a 'low-hanging fruit' service that you can do without effort.

B.   Read the Terms and Conditions of the Tender Carefully

Read the tender document thoroughly. If there is a compulsory briefing meeting, make sure you attend and sign the meeting register, and make sure you have read the tender terms of reference before attending the briefing meeting. This is your chance to address any concerns with the appropriate individuals. If you cannot attend the briefing yourself, send a technical person with an understanding of the bid in question, so that valuable information cannot be missed.

If the briefing meeting is not compulsory but will be held, we recommend that you attend since you will receive insight into what is expected of the successful bidder which will assist you in making an informed decision about whether to apply for the tender and what to highlight in your application to maximise your chances of success.

Choose the method of response, whether a hard copy should be handed to a tender box or an electronic submission. Note that most tenders require a hard copy to be physically submitted to a tender box before the deadline. Read the tender document from start to finish, then carefully complete the tender documents and attach any relevant supporting documents.

I will now unpack the relevant supporting documents needed for your tender document.

i. CSD Document

Print it out and double-check that your preferred address is the one you want reflected, that your director's information matches that on CIPC, and that your taxes are up to date. Ensure that your email address and contact information are current and correct, your banking information is current and validated, you do not work for the government, and you are not banned or deregistered. Check that your CIDB is active and genuine, and that your B-BBEE status is correct. All of this information is covered in Chapter 2 above about the CSD, but you must always ensure that it is correct. When submitting your bid, ensure that you print a full report rather than a summary report so that your information is immediately recognised.

> *NB: Even if you have a valid tax certificate, your CSD must declare that you are tax compliant for you to be appointed. As a result, refresh your CSD after filing any documents with SARS to ensure that the integration between SARS and CSD is successful.*

ii. CIDB Document

For construction-related bids, the registration and valid CIDB certification are critical must-have documents. Most of those construction-related bids will be advertised with a requirement that you must have a certain level of CIDB grading. The grading you have determines the type of business environment you operate in, and to some extent, the level of experience you have. You might have good experience but your CIDB grading reflects a 1, which simply means you will be limited in terms of Rand values of what you can tender for. Below is a breakdown of some of those CIDB codes:

Code	Classes of Works
GB	General Building
CE	Civil Engineering
EB	Electrical Engineering Works – Building
EP	Electrical Engineering Works – Infrastructure
ME	Mechanical Engineering
SB	Asphalt works (supply and lay)
SC	Building excavations, shaft sinking, lateral earth support
SD	Corrosion protection (cathodic, anodic, and electrolytic)
SE	Demolition and blasting
SF	Fire prevention and protection systems
SG	Glazing, curtain walls and shop fronts
SH	Landscaping, irrigation and horticulture works
SI	Lifts, escalators and travellators (installation, commissioning and maintenance)
SJ	Piling and specialised foundations for buildings and structures
SK	Road markings and signage
SL	Structural steelwork fabrication and erection
SM	Timber buildings and structures
SN	Waterproofing of basements, roofs and walls using specialist systems
SO	Water supply and drainage for buildings (wet services, plumbing)
SQ	Steel security fencing or precast concrete

Source: Construction Industry Development Board online (www.cidb.org.za)

Below are the thresholds for different grades:

Grade	Maximum Value of Contract That a Contractor is Capable of Performing (Rand Value)
1	R500,000
2	R1,000,000
3	R3,000,000
4	R6,000,000
5	R10,000,000
6	R20,000,000
7	R60,000,000
8	R200,000,000
9	No Limit

Source: Construction Industry Development Board online (www.cidb.org.za)

If the tender/organ of state says they require a CIDB grade 4, it means grades 4 to 9 can compete. A grade 3 has a limit of 3 million, therefore, already the requirement excludes that grade. This is done to ensure that only capable contractors are obtained, and it's based on the estimates of completing a project of that magnitude. CIDB is currently working on certain limitations that will only allow up to three grades higher to compete on such a project. For example, they are looking to introduce a clause that will allow grade 4 to compete with grades 5 and 6 only. I hope it will be implemented soon and become law.

Another factor that you must note is that, as a grade 4, you cannot exceed R6 million when you quote for a project that needs a grade 4. Grade 5 upwards can exceed that threshold. Bear in mind always that the grading was set for a reason, so don't overlook that factor. Moreover, just because there is a limit, doesn't mean you must maximise it. Quote correctly and do not over-quote/under-quote. Always check what your Quantity Surveyor (QS) is estimating and ensure they don't get over-excited and make you lose a bid that you could have simply won by them building in their fees on the Bill of Quantity (BOQ).

iii. *NHBRC Certificate*

If your company is involved with the building of homes, the law requires you to register with the National Home Builders Registration Company (NHBRC). The NHBRC certifies builders who meet the prescribed industry standards in terms of technical competence, construction experience, and financial capability. The goal is to ensure the protection of consumers against bad workmanship, poor quality material, and substandard houses from unscrupulous home builders/contractors. A valid certificate is issued by NHBRC to a contractor who meets their requirements and must be attached when submitting your bid for housing-related tenders. For more, visit *www.nhbrc.org.za*.

iv. *SARS Certificate*

Although your tax status can be obtained from CSD, it is always advisable to submit your SARS verification pin. You can visit *www.sars.gov.za* for this. Your taxes must always be compliant. If not, at least get a letter from SARS showing that you have made arrangements to resolve the matter and pay whatever is due to them.

v. *B-BBEE Certificate*

Broad-Based Black Economic Empowerment (B-BBEE) is about the viable economic empowerment of all Black people, in particular women, workers, youth, people with disabilities, and people living in rural areas, through diverse but integrated socioeconomic strategies (*B-BBEE Amended Act 46 of 2013*). A startup company is mostly measured as an EME (Exempted Micro-

Enterprise). An EME has an annual turnover of less than R5 million and is deemed to be at B-BBEE level four (4), however, if it is 100% black owned it qualifies for elevation to level one contribution. It is level two if it is at least 51% black-owned. An affidavit or form from DTI commissioned is acceptable for submission.

A Qualifying Small Enterprise (QSE) generates revenue between R5 million and R50 million, therefore it must be measured with the QSE sector code which allocates points according to ownership, management control, skill development, enterprise and supplier development, localisation, and socio-economic development. The certificate must be done by a recognised person or institution registered to provide such a service.

As I write this, the Employment Equity Bill, 2020 was passed by Parliament on the 17th of May 2022 and the President signed it into law on the 12th of April 2023, with the intention of promoting diversity and equality in the workplace, and empowering government to set specific equity targets by sector and region where transformation initiatives were lagging. This will affect some aspects of your B-BBEE certificate. Check with professionals on what the changes will mean to your company or the relevant treasury office within your area.

vi. SBD-1 Document

Standard bidding documents (SBD) are a part of compliance that must be adhered to and submitted when you tender. The SBD-1 is normally an invitation-to-bid document that must be completed with your company details. You need to make sure that everything is completed fully, clearly, and correctly in black ink. This is your front document that informs the organ of state about your company and includes your CSD number, tax pin, contact details, and contact person. The form has a disclaimer that says the bid may be declared invalid if any of the above particulars are not provided. Critically, you must make sure you sign the form and date it. If you are not the owner of the company and you have authorised someone to sign the tender documents, please attach that authority to sign or a resolution to that effect.

vii. SBD–4 Document (Very Important)

This document has been amended by a PFMA SCM Instruction No. 03 of 2021/2022 and replaces the old SBD-4, 8 and 9 documents. It has been in effect since 1 April 2022. This is one important document that must be given special attention. I will allude to you a few things that would disqualify you within this document, purely because attention to detail is not given to it or maybe the person completing the documents has no idea what the content is saying or requesting. It is called a 'Bidders Disclosure Form' and requires certain declarations to be truthfully made. Let's look at the points in detail below:

> **2.1** says, "*Is the bidder, or any of its directors / trustees / shareholders / members / partners or any person having a controlling interest in the enterprise, employed by the state?*"

The form gives you only two options - 'Yes' or 'No'. Now, the challenge is that most service providers just tick or select 'No' without verifying the details of their people. They will insert the CV of a person as an employee of their company, while the person is also employed by the state. It is imperative that you check the employment status of everyone in your company/team because the question doesn't end only with directors. It distinctly states, "... any person having a controlling interest in the enterprise", which could be a spouse.

> **2.2** says, "*Do you, or any person connected with the bidder, have a relationship with any person who is employed by the procuring institution?*"

This clause is checking the relationship with any person who is employed by the procuring institution. So, all directors must declare if they have anyone employed within that procuring entity they are bidding at. It could be a spouse, child, or any other close relative. Concealing such information only for it to be found out will lead to your bid being disqualified. Disclosing this information correctly and honestly will only lead to internal processes that verify whether the person has no influence in the bidding process, direct or indirectly, but it won't lead to disqualification before verifying all other facts.

> **2.3 says, "*Does the bidder or any of its directors/trustees/ shareholders/members/partners or any person having a controlling interest in the enterprise have any interest in any other related enterprise whether or not they are bidding for this contract?*"**

I have bolded the question on purpose because this is where most people hurry to say 'No', because they most probably have answered 'No' for the first two questions and assumed it to be the same for this one without fully processing what this particular question is asking. On CSD, under the director's details, there is a portion that reflects the companies the director is involved with other than the one they are bidding with. It will show the MAAA numbers of those companies if those companies are also registered on CSD. Once you have said 'No' on the SBD-4 form, but the CSD reflects that you have other companies, even if they are not bidding for this tender, your bid will be disqualified. Therefore, take considerable care to watch out for such negligent disclosure, as I refrain from saying it is malicious. Most of the time it is pure ignorance, not reading properly, or negligence.

Clause three (3) of the SBD-4 form involves signatures and declaring that you have disclosed accurately, but if you read 3.2, you will note that it says that your company will be disqualified if the disclosure is found not to be true and complete in every respect. Please make sure that due diligence is done on every document you submit and sign, and satisfy yourself with its accuracy and truthfulness.

viii. SBD-6.1 Document

This is an SBD form for claiming preference points. The form has changed with the current and new regulations of 2022. You have to check the bid to mark the correct scores between 90:10 or 80:20. The critical aspect here is to check and know what the specific goals are and provide supporting evidence accordingly. If they say they want women ownership at a certain percentage, your ID copy/s as director/s must be attached, including the CIPC copy, and share certificates so that it is easier to verify those points you are claiming for.

The information required for claiming the 10 or 20 points is no longer the same. The old PPR 2017 was based on points for B-BBEE, but now with the PPR 2022, each organ of state has certain specific goals. The specific goals may include categories of persons historically disadvantaged by unfair discrimination based on race, gender, and disability. So, you will have to read the state organisation's specific goals carefully and claim them accordingly. In addition, never mislead or lie as the points won't be allocated and you might find your company being reported for possible blacklisting, due to submitting misleading or malicious information. Most importantly, do not forget to sign the form.

ix. SBD-6.2 Document

The form will be part of the bid documents if the bid for goods, works, or services required falls within any of the designated sectors. Certain industries or sectors have been identified as protected against dumping and imports, and therefore when they are procured, certain minimum thresholds for local content must be met. Familiarise yourself with those thresholds and request the suppliers you are ordering from to provide you with information regarding the goods you will be supplying so that you can complete that form. The responsibility lies with you as the service provider to ensure what they are saying is true because it might impact your bid if anything is found not to be truthful.

x. SBD-7.1, 7.2 and 7.3 Documents

SBD-7.1 is a contract form for purchases of goods/works, while SBD-7.2 is a contract form for the rendering of services, and SBD-7.3 is a contract form for the leasing/purchasing of income generating assets, such as property rentals. Whichever bid you are submitting for, one of these forms will be in the bid documents. Just make sure it is completed in full and signed. Note that all these forms have a second part, which is for the organ of state to complete.

xi. GCC (General Conditions of a Contract) and SCC (Special Conditions of a Contract) Documents

All invitations to bid must clearly stipulate the scope of work to be done, the goods to be supplied, the rights and obligations of the state institution and of the supplier or contractor, including the functions and authority of the project manager. All bids and contracts should be subjected to the GCC, and the standard wording may not be amended. You might find that in construction-related projects they use the GCC for Construction works published by the South African Institution of Civil Engineering (SAICE).

If any aspect is not covered by the GCC, the SCC relevant to that bid may be compiled separately, but the special conditions will be supplemented by the GCC. Should there be a conflict between the GCC and the SCC, the condition of the SCC will take precedence. As a service provider, learn to read all clauses of the contract or seek help so that you can understand all your rights and obligations, including conflict resolution, and most importantly, when and how you will be paid. You can choose not to sign the GCC when you bid or you can sign it if you are happy with its contents. However, if you are the winner of the bid, you will have to sign it, therefore it is important that you understand its contents.

Other Returnable Documents

There might be other returnable documents that you will need to submit. Always double-check if you have everything. If there is no checklist provided to you by the organ of state, create one for yourself to ensure that all the requirements are met. Additional documents might include but are not limited to:

- COIDA certificates,
- a health and safety declaration,
- shareholders agreement,
- directors' identity documents,
- municipal rates and taxes,
- SITA-accredited letters for procurement of ICT goods,
- local content annexures when procuring goods that fall within the local content sphere,
- company profile,
- professional indemnity,

- lease agreements,
- share certificates,
- municipal rates, and
- any other relevant documents they might deem necessary.

If you are submitting as a joint venture, remember that all compliance documents for both companies must be submitted including the JV agreement and a joint CIDB certificate when bidding for construction/infrastructure-related bids. When you joint venture, the responsibility is between the parties involved to ensure that their compliances are in order as it will impact the whole submission if one party of the joint venture has some noncompliance.

Functionality

Functionality can be defined as the measurement, according to determined norms (as set out in the tender documents), of the service or commodity that is designed to be practical, as well as the reliability, viability, and durability of a service and the technical capacity and ability of a tenderer (*Supply Chain Management Learner Guide, 2020*).

Most complex projects are advertised with functionality to determine the ability and/or capacity of bidders to execute the relevant contract. It is a risk prevention and safety measure in the system to prevent companies and enterprises with no ability, but with the lowest price, from winning bids. The criteria that will be used in the selection of bidders are always advertised and specified, indicating a certain number of points you must reach for your bid to be evaluated further. It cannot just be assumed after the advert, and it must be part of the invitation.

The organ of state can add any functionality criteria with its sub-criteria relevant to the project. The main criterion normally used to measure functionality include but are not limited to the following:

- **Experience**: It is easy to score points on this milestone and prove it with supporting documents. Just read through how many points will be allocated for a certain level of experience and provide valid documents that can be verified. If you say you have successfully completed a certain number of projects, provide the completion certificates or reference letters that are credible and can be contactable. Do not add your personal experience of where you used to work before you started your own company under the company experience; that information belongs to your prior employers, who might be bidding for this project and may claim the same information under their company.

- **Project Staff Experience/Qualifications/Human Resources**: Always make sure that you read what kind of qualifications are needed. If you submit the CV of your experienced staff, make sure the CV doesn't refer to another company instead of yours. If they are not your consultants, have a memorandum of understanding attached to show that they will be available for the project if you are appointed. Additional to the CV, always attach the certificates to support the qualifications and any legitimate membership certificate that is required. Do not include a carpenter's CV if they are awarding points for a plumber.

- **Financial Resources:** Some projects will necessitate the submission of audited financial statements or a bank guarantee. They will also establish minimum requirements for either turnover or asset value. Always keep your financial statements up to date and your relationship with the banks healthy.

- **Plant and Equipment:** The organ of state will want to know how much plant and equipment you own, lease, or rent, or if you don't own anything at all. Points will be awarded if you can supply supporting documentation such as fleet papers and registration documents for the equipment. Please attach any agreements you have with companies that lease equipment. It must be current and not expired for you to receive points. This functionality criterion is typically used for complicated and large projects, as well as higher CIDB grades. Always ensure that what you claim to possess is reflected in your financial statements, including balance sheets and notes. If you claim to have assets, financial statements will be another litmus test.

- **Methodology:** This is where you promote yourself for these points by demonstrating that you understand the project at hand and how you intend to carry it out. You must include specifics that demonstrate the amount of experience you claim. Include a detailed work schedule and delivery timeline. You cannot, for example, state that you will enlist a house with the NHBRC in 5 days. This will reveal that you have no idea how long it takes to enrol a house. Whatever methodology you use, it must make sense and be practical, and the time frames must be realistic. Show how the resources will be distributed as well. The advertising state organ will normally inform you what they will be looking for in the methodology, therefore, it is important that you read and understand that completely before you draft your methodology. You are allowed to send them questions of clarity when it is confusing, so that you can be on the same page with the requirements and not lose valuable points.

Example of a functionality table

Criterion	Weight	Sub-Criteria	Sub-Criteria Points Allocation	Score as Awarded by BEC/Functionality Committee
Qualifications	20	Doctorate degree	20	
		Master's degree	20	
		Honours degree	10	
		Degree	5	
		Diploma	3	
		Certificate	1	
Experience	40	+ 10 years	40	
		7-9 years	20	
		5-6 years	15	
		3-4 years	10	
		1-2 years	5	
		< 1 year	4	
Methodology	40	Exceptional	40	
		Very good	30	
		Good	20	
		Fair	10	
		Poor	5	
Maximum Score Possible	100 points (Ms)			Score obtained (So)

The bid documents will specify that a bidder must at least achieve a minimum score of 70 points. Any score less than 70 will be none responsive and will not be evaluated further. To determine the percentage score, the following formula is used:

$Ps = (So/Ms) \times 100$, where So = Score obtained and Ms = Maximum score possible.

It is always best to calculate your own score and check if you have qualified with the documents you have submitted.

Pricing

In general, most businesspeople believe that pricing is a major component in tender granting. When it comes to state tenders, price is significant, but it is never the most important element. Every tender will tell you that the lowest bid does not always win the tender and that other factors influence the final decision. This may be true, but having the highest price means you will lose more tenders than you will win. Make certain that your tender is suitably priced. Check and double-check your calculations.

A fixed-priced tender is easy to accomplish since the price is already provided. The hard work comes when you must estimate and price an unfixed price yourself. There is no exact answer as to how to price since each tender is different from the other. However, the clues and details are normally provided in the tender document, and sometimes site visits and briefing meetings will provide you with ideas. The following points must be noted when you calculate your price, but note that this is not comprehensive:

- Do not round off to the nearest number if you know the exact amount you want to quote. A simple example of this is when you want to price R100.94. Put it as such, and do not put R101.00 or R100.00. The small differences you undermine can be substantial amounts that can influence the success of your tender.
- Quote for all items on the bill of quantity. They don't list them for fun; if you are offering them as a discount, state clearly in a separate letter that you will not charge for those services or works but will absorb the costs within the quoted amount. Care must always be given that you are not doing this to win the bid and come back later to contest for a variation order. They will

disqualify the bid if there is not sufficient evidence that you can deliver without impacting their service delivery objectives with a discounted price. It will be assumed that you are quoting to win the bid but have no understanding of what it takes to complete the project.

- If you are VAT registered, always add 15% to your quote, unless the tender has stated clearly that their services are exempt from VAT then you must not charge it. They will most probably provide you with a letter that you can provide to SARS if you are the winning bidder to substantiate why they don't allow you to charge VAT.

- Always tender for firm prices even when the tender is for more than 12 months. If it is a three-year tender, calculate the total cost for three years and tender for that one total price. Avoid tendering with scenarios in mind and assumptions that they will have time to calculate your scenarios or put percentage increases that you also can't calculate for them to assume that will be your tender price. Remember there is a form of offer, and that is one firm price you put in Rand and values, so make sure you calculate everything.

- Do not be greedy and over-quote and neither must you be malicious to underquote. If you know the quantum of the industry you are tendering for, such as housing projects, but the organ of state didn't make it a fixed tender based on the quantum, do not be smart and simply quote the quantum. You might not be able to deliver at the quantum price, since there may be other factors that you need to take into consideration to add on top of the quantum, such as bulk water supply or material access being out of reach and costly.

Form of Offer

A form of offer is a document that is supposed to be completed in Rand values and words. It must match your quotation or the bill of quantity. Make sure it is signed and correctly completed. If you just sign and do not complete the Rand and words values, your tender will be disqualified since you did not offer them anything. There are other documents the organ of state is allowed by the law to write to you so you can correct them - the form of offer is not one of them, since it has to do with pricing and will disadvantage other bidders who made sure their documents are correct.

Bid File

Your bid file represents your company; it is your image and must be presentable and professional. Mark it properly, clearly, and visibly. It is best to have an index/table of content at the beginning of your file and have file dividers for all the returnable documents. If your index indicates that your CSD is inside file divider A/or 1, make sure it is correct and as the index states. A file with no index takes time to evaluate and a lot of information might be missed by the evaluators, even though you have attached it. A neat file that has an index and file dividers and can be verified quickly inspires confidence in your professionalism. If you have heard of the term "first impressions last", then you will agree with me on the file matter.

It is important that you ensure your completed bid documents are put in a sealed envelope or neatly marked file and addressed correctly. Ensure that the envelope/file has the following information clearly written: (a) The tender number; (b) The person to whom it is addressed; (c) The department/municipality to which it is to be sent; (d) The address e.g., room and floor number (if it is provided on the bid document), name of the organ of state, street, suburb, and postal code. These details are easily obtainable on the tender document. In the event that the two-envelope system applies, an envelope/file for Price Proposal and an envelope/file for Project Proposal must be in one package. The envelopes/files must be clearly marked "Pricing" or "Project Proposal" on top and must clearly indicate the bid number. If you submit more than one file because of the information not fitting properly in the first one, mark them 'File 1 of 2' and 'File 2 of 2', etc.

Closing Date

Tenders that are not submitted on time will be disqualified. Ensure you read the tender document carefully and put a reminder on your phone two days before the closing date and time. If your tender is not sent on time, SCM officials will not even open it. Provide enough time for your tender to be delivered to the proper tender box, which may be in a different province/city from where you live. Allow at least 48 hours for a courier service to send your tender if you wish to employ one.

Confirm Receipt of Your Tender

There have been multiple reports of tender boxes being tampered with. My advice is to phone and confirm that the individual for whom the tender was meant has gotten it, then follow up with a confirmatory email. Check the uploaded list of bidders to ensure your company is there. If you use courier services, obtain the slip and proof of delivery.

Follow Up

It is in your best interest to follow up after you realise you have not won the bid. Ask the questions of clarity, not arrogance and entitlement, on where your bid went wrong. This will help you in improving for future bids. Check the website of the winning bidder - they will likely post even their contact details. If they are decent people, they might want to engage with you for a possible sub-contracting so that your business can be afloat and grow, while you learn from them. Remember it is not a must that they must sub-contract you, but you will never know until you try, and by that, you have created a network even for future reference.

Attributes of a Successful Business Person

People who obtain their goals and desires in business tend to possess a number of similar attributes and traits. I wanted to list them below so that you may begin developing them yourself. They are people who:

- Identify opportunities and take full advantage of them.
- Are prepared to work long hours.
- Obtain mandatory compliance with all statutory regulations.
- Make a sustainable yearly profit.
- Embrace technology and learn it.
- Learn and master the art of sales; it is key to any business.
- Deliver as promised or exceed expectations. Excellence is power and it encourages repeat business.
- Satisfy customers' expectations, and respect clients and competitors.
- Pay their taxes and suppliers on time.
- Pay their employees on time and pay them well.
- Treat employees with respect.

- Effectively and constantly market the business.
- Price their products and services correctly and competitively.
- Manage their cash flow and have the skill to keep their business transactions records.
- Try to keep a healthy credit record as they know they will need it to borrow funds.
- Think differently from the masses. They understand that ordinary doesn't cut it in the business world, and you must be extraordinary or suffer producing ordinary results.
- Are visionary in their planning. They focus on at least one business objective at a time.
- Are effective at time management
- Set realistic goals and targets, and measure themselves against them.
- Have the ability to negotiate, especially for buying and selling or renting equipment.
- Know their rights but importantly so, know when to fight for their rights and when to negotiate and not to fight.
- Choose their battles. They appreciate that not everything deserves your energy or fight, so one needs to be smart.
- Are decision-makers.
- Utilise available resources and information effectively.
- Accumulate knowledge and skills, especially financial literacy, computer literacy, and business management.
- Manage relationships with banks, clients, customers, and peers well.
- Are not too hard on themselves, and know that there is always another day to do better.

CONCLUSION

have highlighted what I think is important, and I might have missed a few more things. I would like to conclude with a few highlights about the tendering in South Africa. As we know, most things people complain about include corruption, collusion, tender rigging, favouritism, nepotism, fraud, and all other things. Some things are raised without understanding or evidence. While I am not suggesting that they do not exist, it is unfair to build your business with such a mentality. It means you have already set yourself up for failure without being optimistic.

Not all bids are won because of corruption otherwise, the Auditor General would have long declared the bidding process a huge problem. Just because people bent the rules does not mean the rules are not there and functional. You must master your business, compliance, and marketing. Draft your company profile that has an organogram and ensure you update it regularly since it is your image. If you have resources, create a website for your company so it can be easily viewed and read up on. What I am basically saying is to be professional and stop complaining and being entitled. Effort is important, but knowing where you make an effort is even better.

There will be continuous changes in the government procurement space, like the procurement bill that is long overdue to be enacted. The contentious Employment Equity rules that are going to affect B-BBEE have been signed as well. Government procurement is highly regulated, so, keep your eyes and ears open for any new changes and ensure you understand their impact on your business. If you do not understand, go to the relevant treasury office within your province and ask questions for clarity on those changes. A wise person asks questions but a naïve one assumes the answers or becomes a know it all. Do not make the mistake of being a know it all. Instead, consult, enquire, and even seek legal advice; you can knock and obtain some information from legal experts without even paying for it. Hence, I emphasise that your networking skills must be beyond going around and saying I know a certain SCM official. That is not networking, it is just exposing your business weakness.

Remember you are not entitled to any opportunity; you have to work hard to create it. Opportunity finds you ready for it, working and wearing overalls. This book has tried to prepare you and get you ready for any future opportunities. Treat your business with care and professionalism, and never forget to always network. I know it is not easy when you keep on trying and hitting a brick wall, but it is worth it at the end. Keep pushing without feeling entitled. Keep your mind clear of negativity. Believe in your business and strive hard for it. Get a mentor if you must, because I do not believe there is a person who truly claims they have made it on their own. Somebody somewhere helped you, so be grateful. If you succeed, help the next person, so that we can build our nation to be a better one for our kids, not a selfish and greedy state. Let us rebuild our Ubuntu concept.

Thank you for reading this book, and I hope it inspires some adjustments and knowledge in how you do business with the state.

ABOUT THE AUTHOR

Tebogo Kenneth Monoametsi, an extraordinary individual whose journey began in the vibrant township of Soweto, specifically Meadowlands Zone 1. Currently, Tebogo serves as a beacon of excellence within the Department of COGHSTA in the Northern Cape Province.

With over two decades of invaluable experience in both the private and public sectors, Tebogo has honed his skills as a Public Supply Chain Manager. He possesses an impressive educational background, including a BComm in Accounting and Auditing, a BComm in Risk Management, a Master's in Business Leadership with a specialization in Supply Chain Management, and a Master's in Business Administration in Agile Supply Chain.

What truly sets Tebogo apart is his unwavering determination to tackle challenges head-on, viewing them as opportunities for growth and innovation. He possesses a rare ability to identify, create, and implement solutions through meticulous analysis and collaborative information sharing. Tebogo is a trailblazer, constantly pushing boundaries and seeking to achieve best practices in his field.

Moreover, Tebogo embodies the essence of a true leader. He is not only a team player but also a source of inspiration and motivation for those around him. His infectious passion and unwavering dedication serve as a catalyst for success, driving his team towards greatness.

If you're seeking a professional who not only possesses a wealth of knowledge and expertise but also embodies the qualities of a visionary leader, look no further than Tebogo Kenneth Monoametsi. His exceptional skills, coupled with his ability to inspire and empower others, make him an invaluable asset.

To connect with Tebogo and embark on a transformative journey of success, reach out to him:

1. Email at hello@tebogomonoametsi.com
2. Visit his website at www.tebogomonoametsi.com.

Embrace the opportunity to collaborate with Tebogo and witness firsthand the remarkable achievements that await. Together, we can shape a future filled with boundless possibilities and endless accomplishments.

REFERENCES

1. Constitution of the Republic of South Africa 200 of 1993. 26 of 2005, section 217
2. Municipal Finance Management Act (MFMA), 2003
3. National Treasury of South Africa, Budget Review 2023
4. Preferential Procurement Policy Framework Act 5 of 2000
5. Public Finance Management Act (PFMA), 1999
6. School of Government, Republic of South Africa

Websites Cited

1. Central Supplier Database for Government: www.csd.gov.za
2. Construction Industry Development Board: www.cidb.org.za
3. Easy Tenders: www.easytenders.co.za
4. ETender: www.etenders.gov.za
5. Government Printing Works South Africa: www.gpwonline.co.za
6. Health Shots online: www.healthshots.com
7. National Home Builders Registration Council: www.eservices.nhbrc.org.za
8. National School of Government: www.thensg.gov.za
9. National Treasury South Africa: www.ocpo.treasury.gov.za
10. Online Tenders: www.onlinetenders.co.za
11. SA Tenders: www.sa-tenders.co.za
12. South African Revenue Services: www.sars.gov.za
13. Tender HQ: www.tenderhq.co.za
14. Tender Services: www.tenderservices.co.za
15. Tenderkom: www.tenderkom.com
16. Tenders On Time: www.tendersontime.com